D0274581
00000245101

Exploring Materials

Wood

Abby Colich

Raintree is an imprint of Capstone Global Library Limited, a company incorporated in England and Wales having its registered office at 7 Pilgrim Street, London, EC4V 6LB
Registered company number: 6695582

To contact Raintree:
Phone: 0845 6044371
Fax: + 44 (0) 1865 312263
Email: myorders@raintreepublishers.co.uk
Outside the UK please telephone +44 1865 312262

Text © Capstone Global Library Limited 2014
First published in hardback in 2014
The moral rights of the proprietor have been asserted.

All rights reserved. No part of this publication may be reproduced in any form or by any means (including photocopying or storing it in any medium by electronic means and whether or not transiently or incidentally to some other use of this publication) without the written permission of the copyright owner, except in accordance with the provisions of the Copyright, Designs and Patents Act 1988 or under the terms of a licence issued by the Copyright Licensing Agency, Saffron House, 6–10 Kirby Street, London EC1N 8TS (www.cla.co.uk). Applications for the copyright owner's written permission should be addressed to the publisher.

Edited by Abby Colich, Daniel Nunn, and Catherine Veitch
Designed by Marcus Bell
Picture research by Tracy Cummins
Production by Victoria Fitzgerald
Originated by Capstone Global Library Ltd
Printed and bound in China by Leo Paper Products Ltd

ISBN 978 1 4062 6337 4
17 16 15 14 13
10 9 8 7 6 5 4 3 2 1

British Library Cataloguing in Publication Data
Colich, Abby.
Wood. – (Exploring materials)
620.1'2-dc23
A full catalogue record for this book is available from the British Library.

Acknowledgements
We would like to thank the following for permission to reproduce photographs: Getty Images pp. 7 (© imagewerks), 11 (© John Telford); Shutterstock pp. 4 (© Little_Desire), 5 (© Mat Hayward), 6a (© parinyabinsuk), 6b (© Phiseksit), 6c (© czdast), 6d (© Xiebiyun), 8 (© MC_PP), 9 (© EpicStockMedia), 10 (© wdeon), 12 (© Hung Chung Chih), 13 (© senkaya), 14 (© thieury), 15, 23b (© Amy Walters), 16 (© Mike Flippo), 17 (© wavebreakmedia), 18 (© Ann Baldwin), 20 (© Maximus I), 21 (© iofoto), 22 (© Taina Sohlman, © Nenov Brothers Images), 23a (© EpicStockMedia); Superstock pp. 13 (© Cultura Limited), 19 (© Exactostock).

Front cover photograph of girls painting birdhouses reproduced with permission of Superstock (© Corbis).

Back cover photograph reproduced with permission of Shutterstock (© wdeon).

We would like to thank Valarie Akerson, Nancy Harris, Dee Reid, and Diana Bentley for their assistance in the preparation of this book.

Every effort has been made to contact copyright holders of material reproduced in this book. Any omissions will be rectified in subsequent printings if notice is given to the publishers.

Northamptonshire
Libraries & Informaton
Services
BB

Askews & Holts	

Contents

What is wood?

Wood is a material.

Materials are what things are made from.

Many things are made from wood.

Wood has many different uses.

Where does wood come from?

Wood comes from trees.

Some trees grow in forests.

People cut down trees to use
the wood.

Different trees give us different types of wood.

What is wood like?

hard

soft

Wood can be hard or soft.

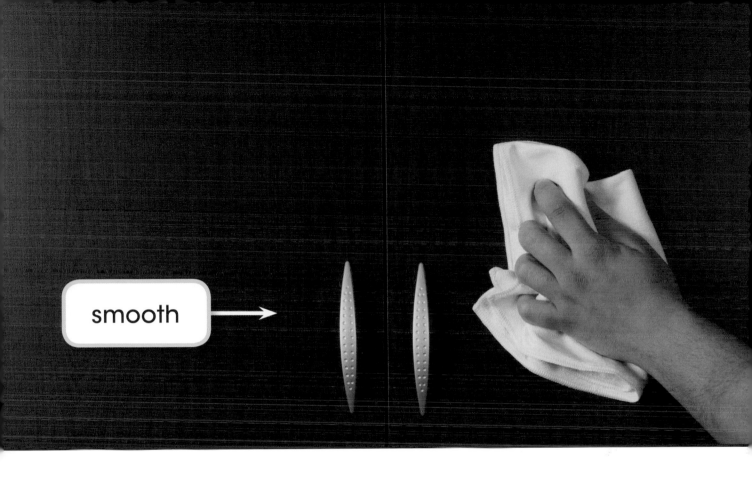

smooth

Wood can be smooth or rough.

Wood can be cut with a saw.

Wood can rot.

How do we use wood?

We use wood to build things.

We use wood to make instruments.

Wood can be used to make paper and cardboard.

Wood can be burned to keep us warm.

Some toys and games are made from wood.

Some pencils are made from wood.

Quiz

Which of these things are made of wood?

Answer on page 24.

Picture glossary

forest large area covered with trees

rot go to waste

Index

The **logs (a)** and **building bricks (c)** are made of wood.

Notes for parents and teachers

Before reading

Ask children if they have heard the term "material" and what they think it means. Reinforce the concept of materials. Explain that all objects are made from different materials. A material is something that takes up space and can be used to make other things. Ask children to give examples of different materials. These may include metal, rock, and wood.

To get children interested in the topic, ask if they know what wood is. Identify any misconceptions they may have. Ask them to think about whether their ideas might change as the book is read.

After reading

- Check to see if any of the identified misconceptions have changed.
- Show the children examples of items made of wood, including clothes pegs, wooden spoons, and wooden bricks.
- Pass the wooden objects round the children. Ask them to describe the properties of each object. Is the wood coloured? Heavy or light? Ask them to name other items made from wood.